AF614168

Free Verse Editions
Edited by Jon Thompson

NORTH | ROCK | EDGE

Shetland 2017/2019

Susan Tichy

Parlor Press
Anderson, South Carolina
www.parlorpress.com

Parlor Press LLC, Anderson, South Carolina, 29621

© 2022 by Parlor Press
All rights reserved.
Printed in the United States of America
S A N: 2 5 4 - 8 8 7 9

Library of Congress Cataloging-in-Publication Data

Names: Tichy, Susan, 1952- author.
Title: North | rock | edge : Shetland 2017/2019 / Susan Tichy.
Description: Anderson, South Carolina : Parlor Press, [2022] | Series: Free verse editions | Summary: "North | Rock | Edge is a walker's encounter with the coasts of Shetland, testing what the lyric can do on the fractal edge between language and "a planet's / broken / openness.""-- Provided by publisher.
Identifiers: LCCN 2021039369 (print) | LCCN 2021039370 (ebook) | ISBN 9781643172767 (paperback) | ISBN 9781643172774 (pdf) | ISBN 9781643172781 (epub)
Subjects: LCSH: Shetland (Scotland)--Poetry. | LCGFT: Free verse.
Classification: LCC PS3570.I26 N67 2022 (print) | LCC PS3570.I26 (ebook) | DDC 811/.54--dc23
LC record available at https://lccn.loc.gov/2021039369
LC ebook record available at https://lccn.loc.gov/2021039370

978-1-64317-276-7 (paperback)
978-1-64317-277-4 (pdf)
978-1-64317-278-1 (ePub)

1 2 3 4 5

Cover art: "Sputsjela" — Peter Davis, watercolor & chalk on paper, 2019. peterdavisshetland.com
Cover design by David Blakesley.

Parlor Press, LLC is an independent publisher of scholarly and trade titles in print and multimedia formats. This book is available in paperback and ebook formats from Parlor Press on the World Wide Web at http://www.parlorpress.com or through online and brick-and-mortar bookstores. For submission information or to find out about Parlor Press publications, write to Parlor Press, 3015 Brackenberry Drive, Anderson, South Carolina, 29621, or email editor@parlorpress.com.

for Peggy

north was here

Contents

Some particular place   fleeting
and fixed

—Susan Howe

60° North | Arriving, Stand Still

if you can, haul-to within

the terms of anguish :

this rough coast a gate

not map, no compass rose

sketched in a notebook

with certain positions

of uncertain objects

marked—as there an eider

dives to protect its

fish from thieving

gulls, & here wind

elevates to a theory

of time : to not miss a single

wave's decay, a verse

of coast becoming dearth

of certainty, to undefine

the edge as noun, dissolving

in the not unyielding mouth

of cliff : verse/reverse

from the root of *turn* :

wind-wave & swell

compounded to a single

force, broken
by the thing it breaks—
re-sounded by the fractured line
it thunders through its own
blow : holes & fissures
you stand above, no visible
storm, just riot in the blues
& whites, the hiss of foam
a light that booms
& edges : wave-rose
of fetch, direction, pitch
as boot reports each wave
arriving, & air-to-water-
to-rock-to-bone
your will becomes
its instrument : to edge
be edged : to give
receive : the far
is here, an eider
in its pool of calm
holding to it, eating
of it, now

60° North | A Coast Severed

from the word
line, fractal
shatter, from stack
to voe, ayre
to wavelet
filling a boot-track or
not quite : impossible
to edge
this serpentine
harrowing
bent to what place
is not—the instant vs
the half-life
of habit—
invasive rapture
so body turns
to habitat : as rock
to root, each
chemical signature
annotates its own
becoming :
who spoke
who turned
& in what wind :

instantia crucis

of continents

colliding, waves

with a thousand miles

of fetch

each stone locked

in its path

of fracture :

here return

no solitary

wound, imitate

with the mouth

the shape of cliffs

or the open/closed

of tides, the sea

& the rock

eating each other

into form—

body itself

as fractal vessel

fractal pause—

& the mind

feels large

simply because

it is here

Muckle Roe | The Mistakes We Make When We Think About It

are all the mistakes we make

when we think : better to sketch

from a moving boat   each thought

hand-held   *contactual*   a mark remade

unbordered   by spliced line

re-laced boot   a northern light

that thickens   thins   till line & color

separate   as if in time   their movements

appositional   like flickering personae

the stage-effects   of cloud & wave

where rock strata   slant from sea

—the boat lifted   the boat still—

& waves break   into cliffs'

water-colored bruise : words

break here   into Gulf Stream

North Atlantic Drift   Shelf Edge Current

diffusing north   as water

carries water   carries air

a climate riddle   *stratagem*   *fleece*

of sheep at ebb-tide   grazing

—defensive   verbal   coastal—

one wavering line   scribble of foam

to carry this little weight   of fact :
what the pencil edges   the brush crosses
as water to land   wind bends left
then slows   & land to water
wind bends right   accelerates—
a breeze on one cheek   then the other—
wash of color   wave froth
of sandwort   campion   silverweed
on shingle cliff-top   careful-footed
a species of exactitude   that rises
edges   step-by-step   the wind-
lapped waves   of a shallow loch
sweet water eighty yards from salt :
red-throated diver   rock-still on eggs
hard-blown   in gravel light
bends your path   as touch of cloud
scrape of foot   separate   then cross
to clarity : cross-sea   back-sweep
afskod of breakers   pulling hard
against the push   of map-line
cliff-foot   penciled beach
that whitens   reddens   whitens   washed
with salt-color   salted doubt

A Path Through Palmer, Ramke, Kettla Ness & Various Unsaid Sounds

Each looked into water

and was frightened

by a different thing—

a pattern or what happened

here : a pile of rocks to mark

a hole, so boot can't break

through seep to salt, nor world

collapse, nor lambs mire

Some seeps are holy

Some lambs die

Some pain can magnetize

the smallest mark

on the biggest map—

lights that burn over wet peat

where carbon sinks like sun

Your footsteps say

better, better

& even on the cliffest edge

a cloud remains

itself : the rain, the wave

will break each other—sweet

& salt—to spell what they won't

pronounce

Beware a thought

untaught by walking :

it looks like land

but water owns it

—*again, against*—

& carbon sinks like sun

60° North | What Is There If There Is No Line

a shatter of sea   *crow-blue*

then metal-bright   as winter sun

clouds   clears   over once-

valleys   salt-light flooded

coiled   from inner coast

to outer—a thousand miles

of salt-path wander   up wicks

& voes   firths & bays : find rock

enough   to stand in the middle

of *bak*   ridge of hills   or *bak*

ridge of waves   what is

& isn't   ocean   is & isn't

soil on granite   starved

to peat   as tide starves down

to map : step *here*   & *here*

to follow wander   *sinder*   twist

through voe   volition

of drowned land   still sinking

its mudflats pierced   by redshank

plover   careless boot   a squint :

noon-sun   low-silvered   hardens

the tarmac gleam   of Skelda Voe

looking as if   *it were not that*

one iron wedge   of Atlantic blue

its *glid*   gull-flit   *saatbrak*   slant

in which dropped things   will rise

rapacious   shored

Carrying Howe Down to Meal Beach

Clear-cry curlew

never-dry slope

its sweetness

channeled

to sort seed-brine

weed-sheaf   inventing

a stray eye :

through aperture   gate

amulet   descend

As white in water

form forms   dissolves

to conjure syntax

a steering of birds

on isobars

& thermoclines

a bottom concealed

by depth   & play

of air *as clear*

as far

It's here you must

exchange

eyes

as listener

on the dreamer's

dream

depends

& salt pounds

each echo back

& back

The being

of Being is will   *was*

both littoral

& literal

a scrawl

of pegmatites in granite

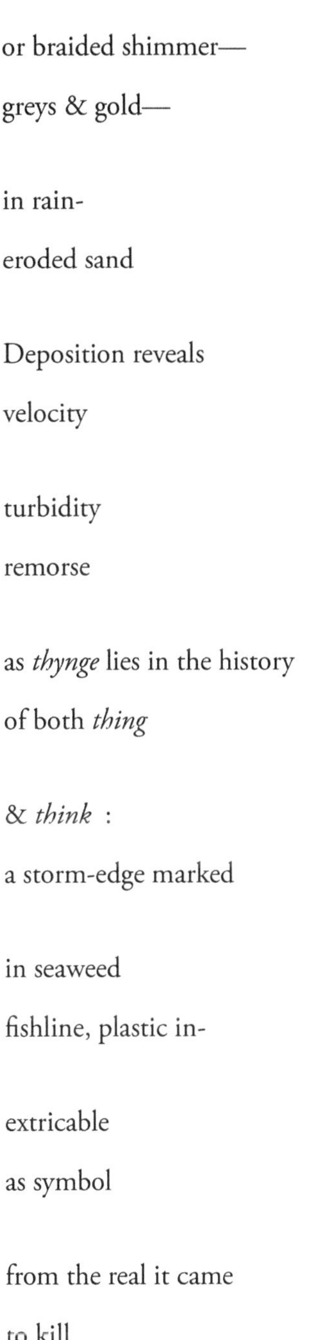

or braided shimmer—

greys & gold—

in rain-

eroded sand

Deposition reveals

velocity

turbidity

remorse

as *thynge* lies in the history

of both *thing*

& *think* :

a storm-edge marked

in seaweed

fishline, plastic in-

extricable

as symbol

from the real it came

to kill

60° North | Tide-Scour

a rusty, uneven

sheen, trading

in tones between

machair & sea

to brush down deep

the grain

of prediction

a light described as

discontent

grew

glided back

as it fell

darted

shimmered

thick

among rocks :

there was, everywhere

a difficulty

fossil pollen

ghost forest

or simply *hill*

cluttered with haze

a hint of air

both south & west

the sun slowly

thickening—

as delicate spine

stretches under

steers in close

a migrant

of permanent storm

severed

vernacular

river or rock

grass-root-sea

fissured

by wings, up-

tilted, a continent

split, upended :

one stained thread

in a tidal pool :

to turn, if turned

resists

light

is silent   whetted

stands unread :

a pulled performance

of shore ceases, wave

by wave, sound

as rock, as rock

is form

lingering, a

small transparent

terror, categorically

permanent, it

toils, repeats this

tide-scour

uneven trade

in search

of surface :

slender beach

no more

than an in-

clination

Hannigarth | Fishnet Wound Through Iron-Age Walls

wild rock photographed   in situ
struck by the tumbled   tame
hand-knotted rope   half buried
where wind winds   tide chart predicts
toxicity & fate   some frail bone
cold hands   adjusting color
in slanted sun : the granite
the quartz   the pale purple lid
of a water bottle : imagine you can
recapture this—a grey
translucency   whole   lost
in dune grass   feathers   olivine-
tinted boulders   blade-cleft wall
in the kelp & *waar* : in stumbled
clarity   slant above beach
each step *put down*   *for itself*
a part, the part   *cognizant*
aware   as wind
is wind   & granite winds
its string through metamorphic
rock : the net means waves
over-wash   remove each piece

by piece : rewind

the sand-lace track   of abandoned

foam   a delicacy among

this wreckage   rising

where oystercatcher   dunlin   boot

with gull tracks cross   the wind-

wave sand : unbury

the advice of iron   the rope

of midnight sun   on north horizon

uncaptured force   of sharpened edge :

through upright stones   a snared light

as if a thought had let itself   be seen

On Foot with Oppen | Muckle Roe

to altar what we cannot alter

unlimited drift stone-on-stone

impenetrable if true this

resistant ounce adapted to the order

of islands their waves & drongs

inhuman lives of the wind

I had hoped to arrive at an actuality

its boundary or prediction point

a single balance forced from three

directions : *to north* (now rare)

a turning or a setting out

—arrival not in the definition—

deeps of granite broken

bloomed cliff path turns

to trace a lochan bench

a hill the stacks cleft

by water govern water

as waves divide then cross

like a wrinkled cloth blue-silver

surface inshore green an arc

which awaits nothing

the fact bewildered bewildering

as each wave beaches   returns
its water   to water : between
red-granite sand   & cliff
a pale drift   wind-blown   shell-light
a fold-within-fold   that does not
repeat   does not   begin
to shield us from open   *time*
a singular wreck   of rock
& step   cold wind above
the footpath   unsteadily moves
& changes : astonishment
that if it strikes us   we are truly
here   *a state of matter*   opened
etched   as lichen jigsaws
a boulder's face : *the force*
of days   light of three seas
to rescue the image   bereft
on its chosen   ledge

Kettla Ness | 'Between *Walking* & *Watching* the Whole World Slips

goes missing'   as cloud-light

drains   through schist

& granite   a vanishing path

of sun-snow   *wadder-ga*

wakening wind   to a noon

dark   original skin

of loch water   riffled black

then silver-black   misspelled

to a clean   thread

pull to unravel   or pull

up path   from mix

& mire   as boot slips

into waste   & waiting

into *waar sea*   & *gravity*

gathering   to wag & wary

wail & wares   as waves

like words   alliterate

begin in sameness   break

on rocks   who

is listening   who will gather

fail & falter   watch & wander

wadder/watter   *wagtail*   *wan*

at *waa*   see *run*   a sea

unraveled   in false sun

of *wadder-biter*   *war* & warn

as wind *wasters*   clears Foula

whitens waves   in the West Geo

washes salt   to the *watter*-land

where words   & steps

wind into one another until   they don't

Skaw Beach | A Turbidite

phrased by reading

vertically

what had been laid down

horizontally—deposition

sequential, upended

its graded layers

a form apart

from itself

track of motion

within motion

of riverbed

on ocean bed

line, mark, shadow, mark

each weight & texture

ledged, aslant

reared up

through sand :

land as a vessel

of vertigo

duration a figure

for grief, grief

a figure for matter

itself, each point

of shatter echoing

a sea before

this sea—

its syntax cut, suffused

by quartz veins

a violence now

within itself

a gleam, a glimpse

of what

we cannot know :

land before fear

as in *prior*

or how

to speak before

a planet's

broken

openness

Keen of Hamar | 'What Is the Name of That Place We Have Entered'

impenetrably ours   the chance

of choice   what language tries

to slip under : *continental drift*

a phrase soft   as sea-fog

fretting force   rock floor so heavy

its valleys create   oceans

knocked by collision   up

& over   continental rock   a wreck

400 million years older than

Pangaea : condense to five words

seventy million years of magma

upended   broken   walk

its shatter   tilted layers

crushed in twist   of thought

—or twisting—caught   as always

in slippage : verb to noun   now

to not : striations white-threading
what the hand holds : sea-green

crystal   crustal serpentine   floated
whittled   crushed in waves

of dunnite   a pinch of motion
stilled in the eye   of the lens

* * *

underfoot   a stumble
break-rock   of dis-placed

time : a small rubble   plain-brown
ice-swept   where deep fracture

drains perpetual wet   implausible
desert   sub-arctic drought

a little core   of nothing
to catch   to keep

a rain   or root : on hands
& knees   the small plants

of mountaintops : to find them
here   their fibers   fissured

through rock   rocked
dull gold   by the bluest

sea   as each wave smacks
its load   of alliteration :

begin as wind   end in toss
afskod   on shoal

& shore   dislodging some
never-to-be-repeated

thought : chickweed that grows
in no other soil   frog orchid

miniaturized   by dearth
self-heating campion   proof

against wind   as a chip of pure
serpentinite   fits in a pocket

breaks the law
of expectation : thievings here

of what we have not

made

* * *

of what   have we made

our dissolution

legible fracture   of words

from things   matter

from mattering : on knee

gravel   wind/rain   face

the sea   & what

disappears   is here

below skin   surface   breathe

its shatter

a tossed cloud   caught

in infinite   displacement

body or sea   each wave a cup

of micro-   nano-blood/brain no longer

barrier   but coast

where light scatters

white-threading   thought

as particle   noun   wave   verb

conjoined   disjoined in fractal

shift : from not to now

sea-floor   stratifies   lithifies

upends unending   fracture

impenetrably ours

where polymers

almost   but can never

dissolve

Hermaness | An Inselberg Is the Hardest Part

of the sea   a paleoform

of slowed rock   burned on

through Dissolution   in cold

friction   brimmed

& ghosting   as whale

or cloud   or merely

color   drifting close

to form : the stinking white

of gannetries   zoomed-

in haze   Whites

of Wheels   to compass

border   haunt   what ledges

stands : metamorphic

cliffs   tilt seaward

dive down vees   of rift

a clear   what-happened-here

before a *here*   to own :

one ocean falling in-

to another   each Verge

white-lined   as blue

meets blue   to roil the inshore

deep—*da haaf*—

where rock column   falls
abrupt   to eroded floor :
from clifftop   listen
find   if you can
a compass sea   *moder dy*
—the longest swells
with longest fetch—
reaching under   wind & wave
to feel the shallows   pull
refract   through *waari baa*
& *baksook* wash   to home :
home in on stealth   of effort
—random forces   random rock—
a not-conclusion   positive
as *baffle*   *beckon*   *puzzle*
guess   this relict seamed
each wave a seemless
molten : in silhouette
un-silent time   sharp-edged
with *now*   & *now*

With Moore & Niedecker on the North Sea | Seeing

that terns & skuas

are *quicker than rocks*

that lichen acidifies

sandstone back

to sand

on the *mossed mass*

of Feadda Ness

& the boat's

white wake un-centers

below white cloud

with pirate skuas, diving

gannets, razorbills

arrowing sea to cliff

shadow-cut & back

to ink-blue chopped

green-silver, *cellar-black*

one pale sea-arch

suspended   paused

where sandstone beddings

tilt & vee—cave to arch

to stack & back

to razorbills, guillemots

diving cliff-shelf

to sea, a seen surface

pierced

& parsed—

our lovely finite parentage—

& all thoughts *spine*

into spine

Walls Boundary Fault | 'To Fill a Gap, Insert the Thing That Caused It'

in this case   rupture

knocked   recalled

as hinder   sunder

sudden   utterance

an interval refigured

as step   as time

as all along

beside   & through

& of   the grassy wet

& gravel   *most*

like Chaos   riddle

pluck   of Evidence

to justify fault-plane ::

between   Despair

& crumble   cloak

of Stopless green   a grass

wind-raised   & razed

grip   the sought thing

& thing unthought :

a sudden fall   of foot

to fault :: approached

light flits   on blue schist

on Quey Firth   a scattered
glare collapsed   collapsing
in mirror wall   of granite
wine-dark   unmoved   its own
Repealless thing : a shelf
of daisies   buttercups in paused
descent :: what small belies
unboundedness   boot leads
slides   *odd Fork* of rock
to beckon   baffle   stun
the beach at bottom   blazed
with kyanite   in schist more swirled
than sea : on boulders   limpets
bladderwrack   here wade in un-
conclusion—all famine   pencil
darkness   banned
by solid bliss   of air

Tombolo | 'Holes in a Cloud Are Minutes Passing'

odds of light

winter-low on the sharp

horizons

of Inns Holm

& the High Klett

remixing foam

where waves collide

collude : at low tide step

where opposing forces

turn—

narrow-waisted beach

pinned by reversed

parentheses of waves

to know what is

& that *it is*

as *knowing*

joins, parts :

overlapping shadows

of doubled surf

reforming

as not-island, not-sea

turning on sand

& turning on sand

where twinned

high-water lines meet

& mark—

their touch dissolving

bitter in

to *bite*

Grind o da Navir | Approach with Palmer, Open Space, & Offshore Weather

did spine write this   did knee   boot

agglomerate   ash   *entirely inside*

the body of another   color of dolerite

weathered or not   color of magma

eaten open : *to cliff* as verb

where sea says   tuff + salt

says *fate*   *kelp*   *nylon*

rope : up-rock the stain

of black algae   foam-cold

at winter's edge   a drift that might

be fog or spray   opened by slash

of gannets   unbearably

blue ice   on Drid Geo Lochs :

follow for a mile   *bound by sting*

cut by tongue   this storm-beach

thirty meters wide   not sand

but boulders   tossed up-cliff

ninety feet from salt : *place yourself here*

as if on a surface   slabbed bedrock

cubed rhyolite   ignimbrite fresh

or weathered   to camouflage

a knee-high blue-green wave-marked

ultramafic : like a lone gull

it pulls the eye answers

nothing : turn round draw bead

on Ronas Hill a red granite

counterlight where snow holds sun

keeps it far as the dark down-sweep

of rain you watch all day but barely

touch : sea-surface lit unstill refracted

like the hard flash of crystal folate

lapped & shear that un-

interrupted rapture as your eye

goes deep & deeper in

to rock : everything broken

reforms & becomes itself

calcite biotite porphyritic

rest *entirely inside the body*

of another : climb stiles lay boot

on pyroclastic flows : as hard

as water wind drags salt & shell

plastic & sand down porous rock

three black domes & the undercut

of a permanent deep Atlantic swell

skuas & fulmars shadow & light

no shutter as fast as *no, then yes*

where matter exists   as blunder

greed   atrocity :: & the wave

when it comes   is energy pure

& simple   white flash of force

in the open mouth   Gate of the Borer

a now here   & a now gone

rock-strewn   cloud-wet   perfection

and at each cardinal point

a murderous calm

Looking with Howe into Holes at Scraada | Rock Cave Where Surf

emerges inland   climbs *irruptive*
a cliff of its own   making   this numb

numb   buffeting   *confined brink*
of wind's uncompassed compass   cut

by noon sun   on south horizon
difficult *to see*   *not see*

this narrow storm   sea-foam
from rock   go back   go back

& whose shatter   under-
storied   undercut   to salt

in air   spray on face   *must not*
see nothing   must not

see *drift*   but sea   boneless
defeating rock   must not

complicit   battle   not
so hurried not   so tossed

as poised :: in clothes

or clouds defeat or feint

to ocean westward hard

with light its cold swallow

swallowed cuts

through soft magma *underthought*

of salt fissure boomed

toward light :: good night

good night good night not long

from noon :: on valiant matter

brain & spine to deafen wind

to stand & walk :: ecstatic

vertical solitude :: emotionless

motionless refuge :: transcorporeal

water-rocked & *not to look off*

but to look

Eshaness | Is It Force or Failure

the moment's quiver

—a wind-forced sea the sea

remembers

in long swells far from wind

cutting rock

as a pallet knife

cuts away

the sheer illogical force of paint

itself—a thousand miles

of water flickering

black/blue

now shoaling turquoise

breaking white   on stacked lava

laced in fracture

the wave & ebb

of rock, now stilled

torn   by waves that nest

in the pure black

in the purple-black
one slice of red in chaos
of collisions : a sunlit boil

strikes & circles
offshore rock
reels off the shattered cliff

to swallow that rock
whole : is this what *nothing*
looks like? a clifftop boulder

pocked with holes
where clast & lava
have parted ways, *events of mind*

impossible
without impact, without sensation
of *thought diffusing*

at body's edge—
the sea-pinks, the fulmars
the lichen, the moss

on sweeps of ash-gray magma
tipped & shattered :
no limit of skin, no pause of need

for the absolute certainty
that rock lives in every cell
that color is

the behavior of light
that words
will not stop turning

into words : all that is made
or cut away, not by wind
that bends the flowers

stings the eye, but wind carried
a thousand miles through water—
the moment quivers

& the hand on rock
takes what rock
takes

& what it gives

Notes

The Shetland archipelago rises from the seafloor 110 miles north of mainland Scotland, at the conjunction of the North Atlantic, North Sea, and Arctic Ocean and within the influence of the north-running Shelf Edge or Slope Current. Shetland's dramatic west-facing cliffs are battered by a permanent deep Atlantic swell with fetch of up to 2,000 miles, so even on a calm day breaking waves may climb fifty or seventy feet above the sea surface. Geologically, the islands are an inselberg, an erosional remnant rising directly from deep ocean floor. *Da haaf*, the deep, can be reached half a mile offshore, at a depth that could take a hundred miles to reach from the coast of England. Shetland's coast—carved by ice into infinite indentations, then flooded by 400 feet of post-glacial sea-rise—winds for nearly 1,700 miles, encircling and penetrating a mere 560 square miles of land. No spot you might stand on Shetland's 100 or so islands is more than three miles from the sea. Long ruled by Norway, Shetland passed to Scotland in the 15th century. Its culture and language descend from the mingling of Norn and Scots, with no Gaelic influence, and all are latched to the sea. The 60th parallel—half as long as the equator and two-thirds of the way to the Pole—marks a borderland where the almost-north gives way to North, a sensation of place impervious to political boundaries, though not to anthropogenic change.

Many of these poems carry shards of borrowed language—intact, shattered, metamorphosed, or intruded. Some words and phrases were sampled by coring vertically through lines—*reading / vertically / what had been laid down / horizontally*. With some exceptions, inclusions larger than a single word are italicized. I apologize for unintentional omissions in the following; chaos will have its say.

The **dedication** quotes the title project of Ellie Ga's *North Was Here* (Ugly Duckling Presse, 2018).

60° North | A Coast Severed derives *eating each other into form* from Bin Ramke's "All Saints" (*Matter*, University of Iowa Press, 2004) and incorporates words and phrases cored and recombined from E. Tracy Grinnell's "dear land" (*portrait of a lesser subject*, Elis Press, 2015). Phrases from the same books also contribute to **60° North | Tide Scour**—from "dear land" *migrant of permanent storm*, and from Ramke's "The Fall/The Unthinkable," *a small transparent terror*. In Shetland *da hill* refers to all nonarable land, be it peat, heather, or rocky turf.

A Path Through Palmer, Ramke, Kettla Ness, & Various Unsaid Sounds begins with lines from Michael Palmer's "The Book Against Understanding" (*The Lion Bridge*, New Directions, 1998), and pulls "again against" from Bin Ramke's *Aerial* (Omindawn, 2012), where it first appears at the end of "Living in Weather." Kettla Ness is attached to the island of West Burra by a fortified tombolo.

60° North | What Is There If There Is No Line visits Marianne Moore's two famous poems of the sea, "The Fish" and "A Grave" (*The Poems of Marianne Moore*, Viking/Penguin, 2003), along shores of the inner coast.

60° North | Carrying Howe Down to Meal Beach cores words and phrases from Susan Howe's "Pythagorean Silence" (*The Europe of Trusts*, Sun & Moon, 1990). The history of *thynge, thing,* and *think* is from Robert Macfarlane's *Underland* (W.W. Norton, 2019) and the OED. Meal Beach (pron. "Mail") is on West Burra.

Hannigarth | Fishnet Wound Through Iron-Age Walls holds shards of William Carlos Williams' *Spring & All*, section IV: "The word must be put down for itself, not as a symbol of nature but a part, cognizant of the whole—" (*Spring & All*, New Directions, 2011 [1923]). Hannigarth is a croft (farm) at Sandwick, on the southeast coast of Unst.

On Foot with Oppen | Muckle Roe quotes a declaration of failure from George Oppen's "Pro Nobis," then laces threads of the subsequent "Of Being Numerous" (*New Collected Poems*, New Directions, 2002) through a summer walk on the coast of Muckle Roe, from Little Ayre past Muckle Ayre and Glista Water onto and beyond Hill of Tongues.

In **Kettla Ness | 'Between Walking & Watching…'** the title, conclusion, and *gravity gathering* are quoted or adapted from Brian Teare's "Olivine, Quartz, Granite, Carnelian" (*Doomstead Days*, Nightboat, 2019) and pays homage to the fall narrated there.

In **Skaw Beach | A Turbidite** italicized phrases are metamorphics formed by coring through E. Tracy Grinnell's *portrait of a lesser subject*, including the sequences "in the frame," "dear land," and "death / is an / innumerable / accuracy." A turbidite is a graded sedimentary bed deposited by a turbidity current. Turbidites exposed at Skaw Beach, Unst, are fragments of a lithified underwater landslide off the continental shelf of Norway.

The Keen of Hamar is a prime exposure of Shetland's ophiolite—a piece of seafloor from the long-extinct Iapetus Ocean. Normally buried miles below Earth's surface, these rocks escaped subduction and were forced by continental collision up and over lighter rocks to form what is now the eastern half of Unst. Continental rocks on Unst's western side were severed from what is now North America when the North Atlantic opened, 200 million years ago. The subarctic desert of the Keen's surface is rare, the geochemistry of its soil unique. The poem walks there with George Oppen's "The Crowded Countries of the Bomb" (*New Collected Poems*).

For **Hermaness | An Inselberg Is the Hardest Part** and **Walls Boundary Fault | 'To Fill a Gap, Insert the Thing That Caused It'** I used both the Johnson and Franklin editions of the poems of Emily Dickinson as oracle books—opening at random, then reading forward and back. **Hermaness** includes mostly single words from Dickinson, italicized or capitalized. I also cored words from the title sequence of Lesley Harrison's *Disappearance: North Sea Poems* (Shearsman, 2020), and pulled *one ocean falling into another* from "Eday, North Isles" in her chapbook, *Blue Pearl* (New Directions, 2017). The **moder dy** (pron. "dye"), mother wave, was the means by which Shetland fisherman could feel the sea under them to find their way home in any weather. What they felt—and could distinguish from local wind-waves—was long-distance swell, set in motion by winds that could be hundreds, perhaps a thousand miles away. Originating in the North Atlantic to the west and the Norwegian Sea to the north, such long-traveled waves display regular length and period, and—most importantly—unchanging direction, pointing with compass precision toward Shetland's coasts. The cliffs of Hermaness form the northern tip of Unst, the northernmost inhabited island in Scotland.

With Moore & Niedecker on the North Sea | Seeing uses Marianne Moore's rhetorical style while pulling fragments from Lorine Niedecker's "Traces of Living Things" and "Wintergreen Ridge" (*The Collected Works*, University of California Press, 2002). Feadda Ness forms the southern coast of Noss, on whose cliffs tens of thousands of sea-birds nest and fledge.

Walls Boundary Fault | 'To Fill a Gap, Insert the Thing That Caused It' pulls from the Emily Dickinson poem it's named for (F647/J546) and ends with a phonetic riff on that poem's ending, "You cannot solder an Abyss / With Air—." Words and phrases were cored from other poems, including "It was not Death, for I stood up" (F355/J510), "One Anguish—in a Crowd" (F527/565), "Our journey had advanced" (F453/J663), "This World is not Conclusion" (F373/J501), and "Joy to have merited the Pain" (F739/J788). The festival of italicized prepositions comes from "107" in Hank Lazar's *Days* (Lavender Ink, 2002). Rocks on either side of the Walls Boundary Fault, an extension of the Great Glen Fault, have been displaced about 65 miles in relation to each other, the western block having moved more than 100 miles south, then 40 miles back north. On the Walls Peninsula, Mainland, the fault plane dips gradually through a wet, flower-strewn depression, then drops suddenly to an open exposure above the North Sea at Quey Firth—sloping down between a granite wall on the east and a crumpled slump of grass-covered schist on the west. At its foot, a crescent of sandy beach backs to swirling, schisty cliffs and boulders, beloved of limpets, lichens, and seaweeds.

Tombolo, Winter | 'Holes in a Cloud Are Minutes Passing' takes its title from Susan Howe's "Pythagorean Silence." A tombolo is a spit connecting two landforms, a beach with sea on both sides and sometimes over-washed—in this case the famous tombolo connecting St. Ninian's Isle to Mainland.

Grind o da Navir | Approach with Palmer, Open Space, & Offshore Weather carries shards of Michael Palmer's *Sun* (North Point Press, 1988) along the wave-eaten volcanic cliffs of Eshaness and ends with altered lines from "That" (*Thread*, New Directions, 2011). At Da Grind o da Navir ("The Gate of the Borer," pron. "grinned") Atlantic storms have smashed a gap at the top of a 70-foot cliff, knocking thousands of tons of rock inland. Rock-bearing waves now funnel through the Grind, though the largest still break twenty feet higher, overflowing the cliff at its original height. Storm-beaches of boulders, tossed inland over clifftops, start well south of the Grind, lining the easy walk north past offshore stacks and arches, deep-slashed geos, sea-caves and gloups, exposed lava domes, and fresh water lochs. Eshaness is one of the most high-energy coasts on Earth.

Looking with Howe into Holes at Scraada lingers on Eshaness, looking into the gloup, or blowhole, of Da Hols o Scraada, formed by a partially collapsed sea-cave. At its open end, 300 yards from the coast, surf roars through the cave's remaining tunnel to break on a shingle beach 70 feet below. The poem carries fragments and concludes with a quote from Susan Howe's "Thorow" (*Singularities*, Wesleyan University Press, 1990), which in turn quotes Thoreau on why he climbed Mount Monadnock. In geology, *monadnock* is a synonym for *inselberg*.

Eshaness | Is It Force or Failure incorporates phrases from *The Sound of Sleat* (pron. "soond of slate") (Picador, 1999), Jon Schueler's memoir of (among other things) painting the Scottish sea and sky. *Thoughts diffusing at body's edge* and the *events of mind* made possible by that sensation were phrased by Robert Macfarlane in *The Old Ways: A Journey on Foot* (Viking, 2012). *Color is the behavior of light* and *words will not stop turning into words* derive from lines in Bin Ramke's "The Naming of Shadows and Colors" and "The Question Concerning Technology" (*Matter*).

Words from the Shetland dialect may be found in John W. Scott's *Orkney & Shetland Weather Words* (Shetland Times, 2017); A. & A. Christie-Johnston's *Shetland Words: A Dictionary of the Shetland Dialect* (Shetland Times, 2014); John J. Graham's *Shetland Dictionary* (Shetland Times, 2009); and other sources on *Shetland for Wirds* (www.shetland-dialect.org.uk).

Other sources vital to these poems include Norman Ackroyd's *A Shetland Notebook* (Royal Academy of Arts, 2014); David Malcolm and Robina R. Barton's *A Photographic Guide to Shetland's Geology* (Shetland Times, 2015); Alan McKirdy's *Orkney & Shetland: Landscapes in Stone* (Scottish National Heritage, 2010); and Ian Napier's "The Moder Dy: Steering by the Waves in Shetland's Seas," in *Northern Atlantic Islands and the Sea: Seascapes and Dreamscapes*, ed. Andrew Jennings et.al. (Cambridge Scholars Publishing, 2017).

Islands visited in the poems include Mainland, Muckle Roe, West Burra, St. Ninian's, Unst, and Noss. Foula lies on the western horizon.

Glossary

Afskod : the backwash of breakers

Ayre : a beach

Bak : a ridge of hills; heavy swell, with wind against the waves

Baksuk : backwash, outward tide

Brei : wide

Drong : an offshore stack, narrow or pointed

Esha : ashy

Firth : a fjord, sea loch, estuary

Garth : an enclosure, a farm

Geo (pron. "gjo" or "gyo") : a cleft worn into cliffs by the sea; if narrow, often a collapsed cave

Glid : glitter, gleam, a ray of light

Grind (pron. "grinned") : gate

Da Haaf : the deep

Hamar : a steep, rocky wall or hill

Holm : an islet

Keen : a rocky prominence

Klett : an offshore stack, a lump of rock

Loch : a lake, *lochan* : a pond

Meal (pron. "mail") : sand

Moder dy (pron. "dye") : mother wave

Muckle : big

Navir : a borer, an auger

Ness : a headland or promontory

Noss : a nose, a point of rock

Roe : red

Saatbrak : the spray & foam of breaking waves; a breaking sea

Scraada : origin uncertain; possibly a fissure or landslip, from Old Norse *skriða*

Sinder : to sunder, separate, disperse; to wander

Skaw : low

Skeld : a shield or shelter

Sputsjela (pron. "spoot-shaela") : a downpour

Voe : a narrow inlet, often very long or U-shaped

Waa : a wall

Waar : large-leafed seaweeds, like kelp & bladderwrack

Waar sea : heavy sea that brings waar to inshore rocks

Waari baa : an offshore rock submerged at high tide, a seaweed-covered rock

Wadder : weather, rough weather

Wadder-biter : a sun dog, parhelion

Wadder-ga : a partial rainbow or sun dog

Wan : to wane

War : worse

Waster : to wester; of wind, to turn westerly

Watter : water

Wick : a bay

Acknowledgments

Deepest gratitude to Jon Thompson of Free Verse Editions and David Blakesley at Parlor Press for bringing this book to fruition, and to Peter Davis, for allowing "Sputsjela" to grace its cover. See more of Davis' work at peterdavisshetland.com. Many thanks, as well, to the editors, staff, and benefactors of journals who first published some of these poems—

The Denver Quarterly: "60°North | Arriving, Stand Still," "60°North|A Coast Severed," and "A Path Through Palmer, Ramke, Kettla Ness, & Various Unsaid Sounds."

Entropy: The Birds: "With Moore & Niedecker on the North Sea | Seeing."

Free Verse: "On Foot with Oppen | Muckle Roe," "Kettla Ness|'Between Walking & Watching the Whole World Slips," and "Skaw Beach | A Turbidite."

Oversound: "Eshaness | Is It Force or Failure."

Under a Warm Green Linden: "60° North | Tide-Scour."

Volt: "Carrying Howe Down to Meal Beach."

Those who helped erode my ignorance include John Slack, Scientist Emeritus, U.S. Geological Service; Jonathan Swale, geologist at NatureScot / Scottish Natural Heritage, Lerwick; and Ian Napier, NAFC Marine Center, University of the Highlands and Islands, Scalloway—I thank you for your patience and beg forgiveness for surviving errors. Thanks, too, to the staff of Shetland's exceptional public and community resources—Shetland Museum and Archives, GeoPark Shetland, Shetland Amenity Trust, Shetland Library, and the Shetland Times Bookshop.

My first trip to Shetland was made possible by a grant from the College of Humanities and Social Sciences, George Mason University, and by my companions—Peggy Yocom, Teresa Cain, and Doug Cain—who magnified the joy.

Lastly and largely: joyous gratitude to Lois Green at Workshop & Artists Studio Provision Scotland (WASPS) and to Shetland Arts for a month-long residency at The Booth, Scalloway.

About the Author

Susan Tichy is the author of six previous books, most recently *The Avalanche Path in Summer* (Ahsahta, 2019), a muscle-memory of a life in mountains, and *Trafficke* (Ahsahta, 2015), a mixed-form investigation of family, race, and language spanning from Reformation Scotland to the abolition of slavery in Maryland. She has written extensively about war and its human consequences, including the volumes *Gallowglass* (Ahsahta, 2010), *Bone Pagoda* (Ahsahta, 2007), and *A Smell of Burning Starts the Day* (Wesleyan, 1988). Her first book *The Hands in Exile* (Random House, 1983) was selected for the National Poetry Series. Her work has been published in the U.S., U.K., and Australia, and been recognized by numerous residencies and awards, including a fellowship from the National Endowment for the Arts. Now Professor Emerita at George Mason University, she lives in Colorado. https://susantichy.com/

Photograph of the author by Susan Tichy.

Free Verse Editions

Edited by Jon Thompson

13 ways of happily by Emily Carr
& in Open, Marvel by Felicia Zamora
Alias by Eric Pankey
Ariadne, A Series by Martha Ronk
At Your Feet (A Teus Pés) by Ana Cristina César, edited by Katrina Dodson, trans. by Brenda Hillman and Helen Hillman
Bari's Love Song by Kang Eun-Gyo, translated by Chung Eun-Gwi
Between the Twilight and the Sky by Jennie Neighbors
Blood Orbits by Ger Killeen
The Bodies by Christopher Sindt
The Book of Isaac by Aidan Semmens
The Calling by Bruce Bond
Canticle of the Night Path by Jennifer Atkinson
Child in the Road by Cindy Savett
Civil Twilight by Giles Goodland
Condominium of the Flesh by Valerio Magrelli, trans. by Clarissa Botsford
Contrapuntal by Christopher Kondrich
Country Album by James Capozzi
Cry Baby Mystic by Daniel Tiffany
The Curiosities by Brittany Perham
Current by Lisa Fishman
Day In, Day Out by Simon Smith
Dear Reader by Bruce Bond
Dismantling the Angel by Eric Pankey
Divination Machine by F. Daniel Rzicznek
Elsewhere, That Small by Monica Berlin
Empire by Tracy Zeman
Erros by Morgan Lucas Schuldt
Fifteen Seconds without Sorrow by Shim Bo-Seon, trans. by Chung Eun-Gwi and Brother Anthony of Taizé
The Forever Notes by Ethel Rackin
The Flying House by Dawn-Michelle Baude
Ghost Letters by Baba Badji
Go On by Ethel Rackin
Here City by Rick Snyder
Instances: Selected Poems by Jeongrye Choi, trans. by Brenda Hillman, Wayne de Fremery, & Jeongrye Choi
Last Morning by Simon Smith

The Magnetic Brackets by Jesús Losada, trans. by M. Smith & L. Ingelmo
Man Praying by Donald Platt
A Map of Faring by Peter Riley
The Miraculous Courageous by Josh Booton
Mirrorforms by Peter Kline
No Shape Bends the River So Long by Monica Berlin & Beth Marzoni
North | Rock | Edge by Susan Tichy
Not into the Blossoms and Not into the Air by Elizabeth Jacobson
Overyellow, by Nicolas Pesquès, translated by Cole Swensen
Parallel Resting Places by Laura Wetherington
Physis by Nicolas Pesquès, translated by Cole Swensen
Pilgrimage Suites by Derek Gromadzki
Pilgrimly by Siobhán Scarry
Poems from above the Hill & Selected Work by Ashur Etwebi, trans. by Brenda Hillman & Diallah Haidar
The Prison Poems by Miguel Hernández, trans. by Michael Smith
Puppet Wardrobe by Daniel Tiffany
Quarry by Carolyn Guinzio
remanence by Boyer Rickel
Republic of Song by Kelvin Corcoran
Rumor by Elizabeth Robinson
Settlers by F. Daniel Rzicznek
Signs Following by Ger Killeen
Small Sillion by Joshua McKinney
Split the Crow by Sarah Sousa
Spine by Carolyn Guinzio
Spool by Matthew Cooperman
Strange Antlers by Richard Jarrette
Summoned by Guillevic, trans. by Monique Chefdor & Stella Harvey
Sunshine Wound by L. S. Klatt
System and Population by Christopher Sindt
These Beautiful Limits by Thomas Lisk
They Who Saw the Deep by Geraldine Monk
The Thinking Eye by Jennifer Atkinson
This History That Just Happened by Hannah Craig
An Unchanging Blue: Selected Poems 1962–1975 by Rolf Dieter Brinkmann, trans. by Mark Terrill
Under the Quick by Molly Bendall
Verge by Morgan Lucas Schuldt
The Visible Woman by Allison Funk
The Wash by Adam Clay

We'll See by Georges Godeau, trans. by Kathleen McGookey
What Stillness Illuminated by Yermiyahu Ahron Taub
Winter Journey [Viaggio d'inverno] by Attilio Bertolucci, trans. by Nicholas Benson
Wonder Rooms by Allison Funk

www.ingramcontent.com/pod-product-compliance
Ingram Content Group UK Ltd.
Pitfield, Milton Keynes, MK11 3LW, UK
UKHW041642190726
13854UKWH00006B/2655